Mercy Triumphs Over Judgment

The Power of Christlike Intercession

Francis Frangipane

New Wine Press

New Wine Press
PO Box 17
Chichester PO20 6YB
England

First UK printing 2000
Copyright © Francis Frangipane 1999

Scripture quotations, unless otherwise noted, are taken from the New
American Standard Bible, copyright © 1960, 1962, 1963, 1968, 1971,
1972, 1973, 1975, 1977 by the Lockman Foundation. Used by
permission.

ISBN 1 874367 96 5

Printed in England by Clays Ltd, St Ives plc

CONTENTS

PREFACE

T his is not so much a preface as it is an open letter to those who suppose I am ignoring the world's sins. By the time you have completed this book, you will have discovered why I cannot side with those who are judging and condemning their nations. It is not that I disagree with their analysis of what is wrong, for the world has truly entered a phase of deepened deception and darkness. My disagreement centers on the way we, as Christians, deal with the evil in our world.

Before I explain my position, let me first familiarize you with my past. It is important to me that you be assured beforehand that I am not simply compromising with the world. I have wept, probably more than most, over the sins of my nation, the United States. I'm not glossing over the mystery of iniquity that seems to continually attach its tendrils around American culture. I am troubled when I hear of Christians, especially pastors, who make a practice of watching movies where sex, gratuitous violence and foul language are part of the entertainment. I don't feel prudish at all when I say that I am offended by the sexually blatant magazine covers at checkout counters. I hate dirty jokes; crude humor is an offense to me.

I despise racial jokes and ethnic slurs. In fact, I am ashamed before God for the history of poor race relations in America and that we have taken so long to begin to make things right. This is a charge against my country for which I have positioned myself in ongoing prayer, repentance and action before God.

I don't want you to think that I am unburdened or ignoring the wholesale cheapening of life in our world, whether it manifests through abortion or with gangs or with child abuse or marital conflicts or when any murder occurs. I remain horrified by the multiplied tragedies of war. I'm not aloof from these things, not in the least. I have fasted over them, prayed about them, wept concerning them and been, at times, sick because of them. I know that it was largely because of mankind's violence that God destroyed the world during Noah's day. My soul is afflicted with the wounding of mankind. I am deeply aware of these things.

When homosexual agendas, witchcraft, New Age cults, "Christian" cults, atheism or paganism are promoted for any reason, it disturbs me greatly. When I see my tax money misspent on worthless "pork roll" projects while vast multitudes of little children are abandoned to a hellish, inner city existence, my soul burns within me. For all these things I believe we need to speak out, to warn and to weep before God concerning them.

Let me also say that I am deeply grieved over the divisions, selfish ambitions, slanders, immoralities, prayerlessness and worldliness that exist in Christianity. I lament that, more often than not, the church has not been an example to the world of righteousness and true holiness.

Indeed, there are many things that have distressed me about my homeland. So, if you are concerned about sin, I am as well. I have spoken out against all these things and will continue to do so. We are united and in agreement concerning the reality of sin and its potential consequences to destroy both neighborhoods and nations.

Forgive me for continuing, but I have not just been troubled; I have been involved in trying to change my world. In the past, I and my two oldest children have been arrested for protesting against abortion. I have published pro-life letters in newspapers and pleaded directly with abortion providers.

Concerning race relations: long before it became a recognizable pattern, I organized a regional-wide reconciliation service between people of color and whites at our city hall. I brought together news reporters and television crews, mayors, police chiefs, and church and community leaders from various backgrounds throughout eastern Iowa. We covenanted with God and our local political leaders that our city of Cedar Rapids, Iowa, would be a "city of refuge." I personally paid for it all. I've been hosting similar reconciliation services throughout scores of cities in the U.S., Canada, and other nations where racial prejudice had left people divided and oppressed.

Regarding the church in America: there are not too many who have done more to help unite Christians than me. According to the Lord's prayer for oneness among His people (see John 17:20–21), in hundreds of cities with thousands of pastors, I have led citywide meetings with no other goal than to humble ourselves in repentance and prayer, and return to biblical, Christ-centered unity.

I'm not telling you this to boast, God knows, but to assure you that what I have to say about God's heart toward our nations is not being written by a theorist or philosopher far removed from such pressing issues. Let me say it again, I believe the church needs to confront sin and injustice. If we fail to speak the truth in love to those who promote wickedness, their blood, according to God's Word, will be upon our heads.

However, throughout my struggle I have not only been made aware of America's sinfulness, I have simultaneously been discovering something about the Almighty. What I have found is not just theological information, it's *revelation* concerning His heart: God's mercy triumphs over judgment. The Lord is good. He is slow to anger and abundant in lovingkindness; He has shown that He will relent concerning calamity, even if there is only one person praying for mercy.

He still comes to set captives free, even nations that are held as prisoners of sin. Thus, my deepest prayer is that, by the time you complete this book, your vision will have been restored to our most powerful weapon in our fight against evil: the grace and love of God. My plea before the Father is that new hope and courage will be granted you in your prayer for your nation. Most importantly, I pray that your soul will perfectly match the pattern of Christ's, who ever lives to make intercession and who stands before the throne as a Lamb slain for sin.

INTRODUCTION

I am an American. Since 1989, some remarkable advances have been made in the church in the U.S. We have seen a genuine beginning toward reconciliation between denominations and races. The prayer movement has simply exploded, with tens of millions of Christians serving God in various intercessory expressions. Prayer has expanded from quiet and intimate to loud and passionate; prayer ministries have taken to the streets and squares of our cities to nearly a million and a half men repenting at our national capitol. Additionally, many leaders have adopted a fasting lifestyle, with great numbers embracing forty day fasts for America's healing.

As a result, violent crime has dropped in the United States to the lowest levels since statistics were analyzed. Divorce, abortion, teen pregnancies and a host of other problems have, in various degrees, also been declining. The best news is that, in a number of places, revival and renewal are beginning to bring multitudes face-to-face with the Living God.

As leaders, we know we still have much more progress ahead of us before God is satisfied. Yet, most of us who are guiding the church in America have reasons to be encouraged. We trust that He who began this good work in us will complete it unto the day of Christ Jesus.

However, in recent months I have watched a disturbing trend in the American church: multitudes of "Bible-believing" Christians have turned angry toward the world for its sins. Anger led to bitterness and began to replace redemptive, intercessory prayer with calls for judgment. Stark unbelief concerning America and revival began to invade the soul of certain leaders; a dark hopelessness concerning the future was settling upon a growing number of Christians.

My goal is to counter that hopelessness with hope. I have written to dispel the darkness of fear and unbelief and to position us, no matter what nation we hail from, at the throne of God's mercy. Not only is my intention to defend what God has begun in the church, but to empower us to fulfill the vision of Christlikeness.

I will say, though, that to write this a new level of courage was required of me. I found, facing me, the vicious anger of those angry with America. Jesus warned that, because iniquity abounds, the love of many would grow cold. There is a psychology of cold love, a spiritual stronghold, that justifies anger and bitterness, and seeks to sanctify them as though they were righteous attitudes. When religious zeal compels us instead of love, we will murder people and think we are doing God a service. That spirit of loveless, religious zeal stands guard over many churches and many souls. You will need to be courageous as well. Never forget: love "bears all things, believes all things, hopes all things, endures all things. Love never fails" (1 Cor 13:7–8a).

Let me also say that I have written to aggressively turn back the spirit of hopelessness. I have not sought to offend anyone; I've aimed my arrows at a dark enemy of hell, not any individual. If, however, you are standing next to this evil spirit, or even in agreement with it, you may find my arrows striking you. Forgive me. It has been suggested that I rewrite this book to present my case differently. I might do that in the future but, for now, I urge the reader to persevere through the first few chapters if they seem too uncompromising. I think the point I make in the whole of this book is worthy of any uncomfortable feelings the first part may generate.

Just as I believe for America, I also believe God is about to awaken many nations. In fact, He has already begun to do so in many places in South and Central America, Africa and Asia; Finland and Norway are awakening, as are parts of Russia. These are all places that no one predicted would experience harvest or revival. Because I see the Lord moving mightily in these other lands, I passionately believe it is not too late for your country as well. How can I say that? *Simply because you are there.*

Revival in a country does not start with the world, it starts with the praying church. It doesn't take many. The one hundred and twenty in the upper room were but a handful. Yet, on Pentecost they met the requirements of God: They were humble, had vision, and were united, praising God and praying for power when the Holy Spirit was poured out upon them. The world has never been the same since.

The power of even one Christlike intercessor can delay God's wrath until the time comes when He pours out His mercy. As long as you don't give up on your land, I believe God will not abandon it, either. The prayer of a Christlike intercessor is the most powerful force in the universe.

CHAPTER ONE

Mercy Triumphs Over Judgment

This is a book about the power of prayer. I believe that redemptive, intercessory prayer is more powerful than prophecy. I believe mercy triumphs over judgment and that the Lord is not looking for opportunities to destroy us but reasons to reveal His mercy. If you believe otherwise, I hope to change your mind. If you think God's only alternative for your nation is judgment, I think you are mistaken.

Before I proceed, however, let me reassure you that I agree there are strongholds of sin and oppression throughout the world. There has been, and currently is, much to grieve over. We *should* be deeply troubled, like Lot, with the "conduct of unprincipled men" (2 Pet 2:7). We should at least be moved to tears, if not anointed action, to see the oppression of sin removed from our nations. Yet, we must remember that our warfare is not "against flesh and blood" (Eph 6:12). The moment we begin to call for divine wrath against leaders or people in general, we step outside the mercy of God. We position ourselves and our country in the path of God's wrath.

Indeed, when Jesus' disciples asked for fire to fall on the Samaritans, He told them plainly, "You do not know what kind of spirit you are of" (Luke 9:55). This is exactly our problem: *Many Christians do not know the difference between a judgmental spirit and the Spirit of Christ, the Redeemer.* Indeed, we are not sent as Old Testament prophets, calling fire and judgment down on sinners; we are called to bring healing and redemption to the nations.

Although our modern cultures are guilty of many sins, we must be obedient to expose those sins as we warn of impending judgment. Only One is worthy to call for wrath: the slain Lamb standing at God's throne (see Rev 5). Until He opens the book, we must pray for mercy; until we become lamb-like, our judging is misguided.

This does not mean we should minimize the wantonness that has spread through our society into the world. Sin cannot be glossed over or ignored. Yet, it is precisely *because* sin is utterly vile that we must embrace our role as intercessors who stand and plead with God for mercy.

Intercession is the essence of the life of Christ. His coming to earth and dying for sins was one extended act of intercession. Jesus beheld the depravity of mankind's sin. He examined it carefully in all of its offensiveness, perversity and repulsiveness. But the wonder of the gospel is that, in spite of mankind's sin, God deeply loved the world, so much so that He sent His Son to die for us. We are called to follow this same amazing pattern of mercy.

We are not minimizing sin when we maximize Christ's mercy. We are not white-washing sin; we are blood-washing it.

James tells us, "mercy triumphs over judgment" (James 2:13). To live the life of mercy plays perfectly into God's heart. Mercy precisely fulfills the divine purpose: to transform man into the Redeemer's image.

IDENTIFIED WITH SINNERS

Throughout His life, Jesus reached out to people who were rejected by others. He loved those who were despised, scorned and excluded. Yet, His practice of dining with known evildoers offended the Pharisees, and they confronted Jesus' disciples:

> "Why is your Teacher eating with the tax-gatherers and sinners?" —Matt 9:11

When Jesus heard the question, He answered,

> "It is not those who are healthy who need a physician, but those who are sick. But go and learn what this means, 'I desire compassion, and not sacrifice,' for I did not come to call the righteous, but sinners." —Matt 9:12–13

He told the self-righteous to go and learn what God meant when He said, "I desire compassion (mercy), and not sacrifice." A religion without love is an abomination to God. The church needs to learn that God desires love and compassion, not merely an adherence to ritual and sacrifice.

THE HOUSE OF PRAYER

Jesus said His Father's house would be a "house of prayer for all the nations" (Mark 11:17). True prayer is born of love and comes in the *midst* of sin and need. It comes not to condemn but to cover. All nations sin. All cultures have crises. Yet, these times can become turning points if, in the time of distress, intercessors cry to God for mercy. Thus, prayer brings redemption from disaster.

The church is created, not to fulfill God's wrath, but to complete His mercy. Remember, we are called to be a house of prayer *for* all nations. Consider passionately this phrase: "prayer for." Jesus taught, "pray for" those who persecute and mistreat you. When Job "prayed for" his friends, God fully restored him (Job 42). We are to "pray for" the peace of Jerusalem (Ps 122:6), and "pray for" each other, that we may be healed (James 5:16). Paul tells us that God desires all men to be saved. Therefore, he urges that "entreaties and prayers . . . be made on behalf of all men, for kings and all who are in authority" (1 Tim 2:1–2).

"But," you argue, "My country is a modern manifestation of ancient Babylon." I don't think so. But even if it was, when the Lord exiled Israel to Babylon, He didn't order His people to judge their new cities. Rather, He commanded, "Seek the welfare of the city where I have sent you . . . and pray to the Lord on its behalf; for in its welfare you will have welfare" (Jer 29:7).

Over and over again the command is to pray *for,* not against; not vindictively, but mercifully; not condemningly, but compassionately, appealing to God to bring forgiveness and redemption. The problem is that too many Christians have become disciples of the cynical news media of their nations rather than followers of Jesus Christ. We think conforming to our political party is the same as attaining the standards of God. More often, it is not.

Study Isaiah 53. It reveals in wondrous detail the Savior's nature: Christ numbered Himself *with* sinners. He interceded *for* transgressors. He is "with" us and "for" us, even when He must reveal to us our iniquity.

But the world sees a church with rocks in its hands looking for adulterers and sinners. We have become the "church of the angry Christians." In the drama that is unfolding in the world today, we have not been playing the role of Christ, but rather the part of the Pharisees. Let us drop the rocks from our hands, then lift our hands, without wrath, in prayer to God (1 Tim 2:8).

PRAYER FOR OUR LEADERS

God does not want us to be judgmental; He wants us prayer-mental. As instinctively as we judge people, we should pray for them instead. Today, countless Christians are angry with their elected officials. We say our anger is "righteous indignation." Really? Jesus expressed "righteous indignation" for, perhaps, three to four hours during His ministry. Once was for the hardness of people's hearts, and the other two times were at the temple when the Father's house was used for something other than redemptive prayer (Mark 11:17). How long has your anger lasted? Are you sure your love has not grown cold? Are you sure you are not seeking to justify a root of bitterness?

"Well," some argue, "our government officials have sinned." When Paul called for prayer for kings in 1 Timothy 2, Nero was emperor of Rome. Nero was one of the most corrupt men that ever lived. He did not have an illicit relationship or two, he had public orgies. At night he illuminated his banquets with living torches— Christians, who were tarred and then set ablaze on poles while Nero and his guests dined! Yet, Paul wrote, "Pray for kings and all who are in authority."

Some may misread my words, assuming I think there is nothing wrong in government or society. Yes, there are many things wrong in our world, and God will certainly call us, at various times, to confront the sins that plague our lands. However, my concern is not as much with the House of Lords as with the house of the Lord! If we are not praying for our elected officials, the least we can do is to stop cursing them! As it is written, "You shall not speak evil of a ruler of your people" (Acts 23:5). The Father's house is to be a house of prayer for kings and all in authority. It must also become a source of redemptive intercession for imperfect leaders who sin.

I can understand the reason for anger towards elected officials, especially when we consider that they are not doing their job. But by not praying for them, we are not doing our job. It is not the Holy Spirit within us that calls for God to judge our nation; it is our frustration with people. My friend, when judgment comes, we should realize that it begins "with the household of God" (1 Pet 4:17). To pray for God to judge our nation for its sins actually initiates judgment on the church for *its* sins! And God will start with those who are quickest to judge others.

When I pray for the President of the United States, I ask the Lord to protect him from the influence of ungodly counsel. Where the President has failed, I appeal to God to forgive him, especially for tolerating abortion and late-term abortion. Yet, I also acknowledge that God has done good things through the President, and I am thankful to the Almighty for those things. Have our leaders done everything perfectly? No, but neither have we.

In the *G–A–P*

I believe Jesus Christ is reaching to national leaders like never before. If we pray correctly, we will see a divine transformation come both to these leaders and to our nations.

So many Scriptures compel us to prayer that we should not need any further encouragement to do so. Yet, let me share an experience I had concerning intercession for President Bill Clinton.

In December of 1998, family matters took me to Davenport in Scott County, Iowa. As I entered the city, I was listening to a teaching on tape and had just heard, "We need to stand in the gap for President Clinton." Immediately, a car pulled in front of me from the left lane. Next to the three numbers on its license plate were the letters *G–A–P*. Below the word *GAP* was the name of a county north of Scott where the plate was issued: Clinton.

If that was not enough, three seconds later, a pickup truck passed me on the right and pulled alongside the car in front. It too was from Clinton County. Unbelievably, next to its numbers were the same three letters: *G–A–P*.

Within no more than thirty seconds, as I heard the words, "stand in the gap for President Clinton," two vehicles appeared with exactly the same words on their plates: *GAP–Clinton!*

The Bible tells us that "every word will be confirmed by two or three witnesses." I know that this renewed prayer focus is not just a "fresh teaching"; to me, it is a revealed word from God, confirmed by the Holy Spirit through three witnesses.

The Lord desires us to stand in the gap, positioning ourselves between the failings of man and the sufficiency and forgiveness of God. Then, He calls us to persevere in this intercession until full transformation comes.

For all who are embittered with their nation's leaders, remember: Each of us must give an account for our sins at the judgment seat of Christ (2 Cor 5:10). Let us consider with holy fear the warning of God: "judgment will be merciless to one who has shown no mercy; mercy triumphs over judgment" (James 2:13).

Let's pray: *Father, I ask You to forgive me for my unforgiveness toward our elected officials. Lord, I ask You to forgive, cleanse and renew them in Your mighty Presence. Appear to them, Lord, in the night hours; save them from the lies and plans of hell. Touch and heal their families and renew them as well in Your love. Lord, I ask You to forgive my harshness toward all who have offended me. Oh God, this day deliver me from my judgmental attitudes! Help me to remember in all things and at all times that mercy triumphs over judgment!*

CHAPTER TWO

GRACE AND TRUTH

I have been pleading for a merciful church. How merciful should we expect to become? Jesus said, "Be merciful, just as your Father is merciful" (Luke 6:36). Here is what the Father did in His mercy: He sent His only begotten Son to die for our sins. We are to reach for nothing short of the nature of Christ who, instead of destroying His enemies, died for them.

At the same time, the Living God does not withhold from us revelation of what we have done wrong. Central to the mission of the Holy Spirit is bringing conviction to mankind concerning "sin, and righteousness, and judgment" (John 16:8). If we are to be merciful, even as the Father is merciful, we must also be prepared to speak in defense of righteousness.

Certainly there are times when we must warn God's people of impending judgments—but we must do so without personal wrath or bitterness. There are times when we are called to proclaim from the rooftops the truths of God, no matter how hard the message God has given us—but such proclamations must not be judgmental or self-righteous.

The mercy of God truly is served when we can say to one who has sinned, "What you have done is wrong, but God indeed offers opportunities for redemption." When called to correct, we must learn how to present ourselves to sinners "in a spirit of gentleness, each one looking to [ourselves], lest [we] too be tempted" (Gal 6:1).

Indeed, the redemption of God is ill-served if we fail to warn the world of its sin. If I see someone about to cross a street and they do not notice a car bearing down upon them, my warning is an act of love, not criticism. So also, our warnings to those about to be destroyed by sin must likewise be acts of love, not anger. Indeed, we know how greatly Jesus loved His disciples, yet in His love there were times when He needed to correct or even rebuke them.

Again, when Christ evaluated the churches in the book of Revelation, He did not withhold from them reproof. However, He also presented hope, as well as promise, encouragement and acknowledgment of what virtues each had attained. If all we present to sinners are their failings, without acknowledging the good things God has given them, I doubt that we are representing Christ in our correction.

Thus, God is not asking us to be silent in the face of sin, but to communicate the full spectrum of Jesus' heart: to appreciate virtue when we see it and to give encouragement where it's needed. The life of a mature Christian can speak the "truth in love" and communicate as much love as truth (Eph 4:15). Yet, even when people do not repent, He asks us to abide in Christlike intercession for sinners. Remember: A Christian is to pour out life, not minister death, which is what happens when we speak with bitterness and anger.

The Scriptures tell us that "grace and truth" are realized in Jesus Christ (John 1:17). Jesus did not condemn Jerusalem even as He warned it of coming judgments. He did not just scold the city for what was wrong; He wept over it. He communicated deep love for Jerusalem even as He addressed the consequences of the people's sin.

Christ alone must be our model. We must avoid emulating angry, politically disappointed Christians; our goal is to represent Jesus. Indeed, our openness to the nature of Christ diminishes the longer we harbor unforgiveness and bitterness. Our hearts will become hard. We become hard. It is in this regard that Jesus has a warning for us today. He says, "because lawlessness is increased, most people's love will grow cold" (Matt 24:12).

It would be a great deception to imagine that we are immune from cold love. Remember: The moment we enter the realm of unforgiveness, our capacity to love begins to diminish.

I know of many Christians who, to this day, refuse to go to church or are without Christian fellowship because they were hurt by something someone did in church.

Here is how Jesus told us to handle offenses. He said,

"And if your brother sins, go and reprove him in private; if he listens to you, you have won your brother.

"But if he does not listen to you, take one or two more with you, so that by the mouth of two or three witnesses every fact may be confirmed.

"And if he refuses to listen to them, tell it to the church; and if he refuses to listen even to the church, let him be to you as a Gentile and a tax-gatherer." —Matt 18:15–17

Often, if we do not go directly to the person whom we feel has committed a sin, anger soon begins to seethe within us. The word *seethe* originally meant to "soak or saturate in a liquid." In time, it came to mean to "boil." Today, both definitions fit. The offense we feel becomes an issue that soaks in our thoughts and steadily rises to a boil in our spirits. We may have suffered a genuine injustice; however, seething is not one of the fruits of the Holy Spirit.

Whether or not we are able to speak immediately with the person who is in sin, we must always go first to the Lord. King James renders the above warning from Matthew 24 like this: "because iniquity shall abound, the love of many shall wax cold." Yet, consider: Paul also tells us that "where sin increased, grace abounded all the more" (Rom 5:20). So, we have a choice: either let our hearts harden with anger or find grace that is greater, more powerful, than sin.

John tells us, "If anyone sees his brother committing a sin not leading to death, he shall ask and God will for him give life to those who commit sin . . . " (1 John 5:16a). In truth, the very first place we should go when we are offended with sin is to the Lord. It is there that we find the correct attitude to respond with grace to the sinner's condition.

Having said that, the best time to talk to people about their sin is *after* God has talked to us about our attitudes. When we speak to them of what we perceive to be wrong in them, it must be mercy speaking in humility, not wrath expressed in self-righteousness. Our call in proclaiming the Word of God is to represent Jesus Christ in all things. His nature is the perfect embodiment of both grace and truth.

Lord, show me how to be motivated by love, compelled by mercy and consumed with redemption, even while I speak the truth to the disobedient and sinners. Help me, Lord, to be as concerned about grace as I am about truth, that I might fully reveal Your heart when I speak.

CHAPTER THREE

WHAT ARE YOU BECOMING?

And when day came, He called His disciples to Him; and chose twelve of them, whom He also named as apostles: Simon, whom He also named Peter, and Andrew his brother; and James and John; and Philip and Bartholomew; and Matthew and Thomas; James the son of Alphaeus, and Simon who was called the Zealot; Judas the son of James, and Judas Iscariot, who became a traitor.   —Luke 6:13–16

J udas Iscariot had traveled both with Jesus and His disciples. Along with the others, Judas had been used mightily to "heal the sick, raise the dead, cleanse the lepers [and] cast out demons" (Matt 10:8). He knew the excitement, joy and power of walking with Jesus. Judas was numbered among the original twelve.

Yet, Judas had a serious character flaw, a moral weakness. The Scripture reveals that, despite the fact that God was using him, Judas "was a thief, and as he had the money box, he used to pilfer what was put into it" (John 12:6).

It is significant, my friend, that Jesus allowed a thief to carry the money box. Sometimes we think the Lord is going to challenge us on every issue, but there are times when His *silence* about our repeated sin is His rebuke. Judas knew what he was doing was wrong, but since Jesus didn't directly confront him, he minimized the severity of his iniquity. Perhaps he rationalized that, if pilfering was truly bad, God would not still use him to work miracles.

How a little leaven leavens the whole lump! A relatively minor sin left unattended can lead to a major sin that destroys our lives. Judas "became a traitor." He started out in ministry loyal to Jesus, but then began lying about the finances until his deceitful exterior completely hid a very corrupt interior. Judas was a thief who became a traitor, eventually taking his own life. His unrepentant compromise went from bad to worse, and it destroyed him.

Today, Christians look at the world and see injustice, immorality and corruption. The anger we feel because of these things is not only understandable, it's justified. Why shouldn't we be angry at what we see? Indeed, in many instances we are actually watching hell manifest itself through people and situations in the world!

Knowing we would grieve over the evil in the world, God's Word tells us, "Be angry, and yet do not sin" (Eph 4:26). We must discern at what point anger festers into sin. Paul continues, "do not let the sun go down on your anger."

We can be legitimately angry about things that are truly wrong, but by sundown our indignation must find a more noble, redemptive attitude of expression. We must reach for forgiveness, intercessory prayer, and a love that covers a multitude of sins. Otherwise, Paul warned, we will "give the devil an opportunity" (Eph 4:27). What happens when we do not allow the Holy Spirit to transform our frustrations? Self-righteousness begins to manifest in our souls. We become embittered and judgmental. We become cynics. The definition of a cynic is "a habitual doubter." Do you know any Christians who are cynical?

The worst thing that happens when we turn angry and cease praying is that we, like Judas, betray Christ. How? When we disown Christ's mission of intercession, redemption and forgiveness, we turn our backs on sinners destined to hell.

Judas mutated from an apostle into a person he never intended: he *became* a traitor. Our anger, left unattended, will do the same to us. It causes us to degenerate into something we never planned on becoming: "Christian Pharisees." By allowing self-righteousness and judgmentalism to grow in the soil of unrepentant anger, we become *worse* in God's eyes than the evil which offended us.

Today, the church is overstocked with angry Christians. What can we do? We must turn indignation into intercession. We must make our heartache work for us, aligning ourselves with Christ in the prayer of redemption. Otherwise, we betray Christ's purpose with our anger.

"IT'S THE PRINCIPLE"

I know Christians who refuse to surrender their anger to God in many different situations. These are folks who love their country, possess high morals and seek to walk in integrity, yet feel perfectly justified being embittered about certain situations! Under the guise, "it's the principle," they are completely unalarmed by their unchristlike attitudes.

Where in the Bible does God permit Christians to hold hatred and unforgiveness against anyone? When was it that God gave permission to Jesus' followers to remain angry towards a person for months, or even years?

Thank God, Jesus didn't look down from the cross at the Pharisees and say, "You need to be taught a lesson. I love you, but it's the principle." No. He prayed, "Father, forgive them." And then, amazingly, He *covered* their sin, saying, "They do not know what they are doing" (Luke 23:34).

The sense of Christian indignation infiltrating the church has not come from heaven. James clearly tells us that "the anger of man does not achieve the righteousness of God" (James 1:20). Don't dismiss your anger as a little sin; it disqualified Moses from entering the Promised Land!

It's time to deal with the indignation and unforgiveness. It is a terrible witness to the non-Christian world. You see, even though the unsaved don't know much about the Scriptures, they still possess a God-given sense of who Christ is when it comes to real life issues. Before they will join a church, they are watching how Christians deal with imperfect people.

There are things at stake that are bigger than our indignation about right and wrong. The world is watching how we relate to those who are morally *wrong*, even when we are biblically *right*. And they are watching to see if we look and sound like the Savior or like the Pharisees.

Yet, there is one thing more crucial than how the world sees us, and that is how Christ sees us. He is watching what is happening to our hearts. He asks each of us a simple question: Do you know what you're becoming?

Lord Jesus, help me! When did I switch from loving to judging? When did I replace the glow, the smile of Your love, with this unceasing, angry frown? Master, like Judas, I have become what I never set out to be: a traitor to Your redemptive purpose. Forgive me. Cleanse me of my anger and pride. Restore my heart until I love as You have loved me, until I stand for others in their need as You have stood for me in mine. For Your glory. Amen.

CHAPTER FOUR

ONE MAN

A number of Christians have been saying, "If God doesn't destroy my nation, He will have to apologize to Sodom and Gomorrah." If we accept the premise that Sodom and Gomorrah represent the pattern of wickedness, then Abraham should be for us the pattern of righteousness.

What am I talking about? I am referring to the fact that when Abraham was confronted with the imminent possibility of Sodom's destruction, he did not jump on the "Destroy Sodom" bandwagon; instead, he went before the Lord and prayed for mercy for the city.

Abraham's prayer is an amazing study on the effect a mercy-motivated intercessor has on the heart of God. It tells us that the Lord is actually looking for a spark of hope, a mercy reason, to justify delaying His wrath.

Let's examine how the Lord responded to the sin of Sodom. First, He showed Abraham, His servant, what He was about to do. Why? Because God desired Abraham to intercede. When the Lord informed His servant of what was wrong in the world, it was not so he could judge it, but so that he would intercede for mercy. Remember, God *delights* in mercy and takes no pleasure in the death of the wicked (Micah 7:18, Ezek 33:11). The Lord *always* seeks for opportunities of mercy.

Therefore, let's take note of how Abraham approached the Almighty:

> Then the men turned away from there and went toward Sodom, while Abraham was still standing before the Lord. And Abraham came near and said, "Wilt Thou indeed sweep away the righteous with the wicked? Suppose there are fifty righteous within the city; wilt Thou indeed sweep it away and not spare the place for the sake of the fifty righteous who are in it?
>
> "Far be it from Thee to do such a thing, to slay the righteous with the wicked, so that the righteous and the wicked are treated alike. Far be it from Thee! Shall not the Judge of all the earth deal justly?"   —Gen 18:22–25

Notice, Abraham did not pray from a place of anger. He never said, "God, it's about time You killed the perverts." Somehow, we have come to believe that non-compromising Christians must also be angry. Abraham never compromised with Sodom's depraved culture, yet he was above fleshly reaction. In fact, throughout his prayer, Abraham did not even remind the Lord of what was wrong in Sodom. He appealed, instead, to the mercy and integrity of the Lord.

This is vitally important for us, because Jesus said, "If you are Abraham's children, do the deeds of Abraham" (John 8:39). One of Abraham's most noteworthy deeds involved his intercessory prayer for Sodom, the most perverse city in the world!

Abraham first acknowledged the Lord's integrity, then he spoke to the Lord's mercy.

"Suppose there are fifty righteous within the city; wilt Thou indeed sweep it away and not spare the place for the sake of the fifty . . ."

The Lord knew that it would be unjust to slay the righteous with the wicked; Abraham's prayer did not enlighten the Lord of some unknown fact. But the nature of life on earth is this: *God works with man to establish the future and, in the process of determining reality, He always prepares a merciful alternative.* In other words, urgent, redemptive prayer shoots straight through the mercy door to God's heart. This door is never shut, especially since we have a High Priest, Jesus Christ, ministering at the mercy seat in the heavenlies. It is open any time and every time we pray. Listen to how the Lord answered Abraham's prayer for mercy:

"If I find in Sodom fifty righteous within the city, then I will spare the whole place on their account." —Gen 18:26

How the truth of God's mercy flies in the face of those so eager to judge their nation! Incredibly, the Lord said He would spare the whole of Sodom if He found fifty righteous people there. Now, keep this in mind, the

Hebrew word for *spare* means more than "not destroy," it also means "to forgive or pardon."

This is a tremendous revelation about the Living God: *He will minimize, delay, or even cancel a day of reckoning as long as Christ-inspired prayer is being offered for sinners!*

Time and again throughout the Scriptures the Lord proclaims an ever-present truth about His nature: He is "slow to anger, and abounding in lovingkindness" (Ex 34:6). Do we believe this? Here it is, demonstrated right in the sacred Scriptures. He tells us plainly that a few righteous people scattered in a city can preserve that area from divine wrath.

Abraham knew the love of God. They were intimate friends. Abraham, in truth, had a clear view into the heart of God based on his own experience. This interceding prophet had seen the Almighty bless, prosper and forgive him; he pressed God's mercy toward its limits:

"What if there are forty?"

The Lord would spare it for forty.

Abraham bargained, "Thirty?"

He would spare it for thirty.

"Twenty?"

He finally secured the Lord's promise not to destroy the city if he could find just ten righteous people there. Think about this, for herein we discover the heart of God: *The Lord would spare sinful Sodom for the sake of ten godly people who dwelt within it!*

HOW ABOUT YOUR COMMUNITY?

Now, let's think of your city: Are there ten good folk among you? Consider your region: Do you think there might be one hundred praying people living within its borders, people who are pleading with God for mercy? What about nationwide? Do you suppose there might be ten thousand people interceding for your country? God said He would spare Sodom for ten righteous people. Do you think God would spare your nation for ten thousand righteous?

I live in a metropolitan area in the U.S. that has about two hundred thousand people. I can list by name scores of individuals, including pastors, intercessors, youth workers, black folks, white folks, Hispanic folks, native Americans, Asian Americans, Christian business people, moms, dads, godly teenagers, praying grandmothers, secretaries, righteous policemen and on and on—far more than the ten righteous needed to save a place like Sodom. There are many here who care for this city.

Think about your church and the greater church in your city. Are there at least ten honorable people who sincerely care about your community? The Lord said He would spare Sodom for the sake of the ten.

JUST ONE

Abraham stopped praying at ten. But I will tell you something that is most profound: *Abraham stopped too soon.* The Lord reveals that His mercy will extend even further. Listen to what He told Jeremiah:

Roam to and fro through the streets of Jerusalem,
and look now, and take note. And seek in her
open squares, if you can find a man, if there is
one who does justice, who seeks truth, then I will
pardon her.   —Jer 5:1

He says, "if you can find a man . . . then I will pardon
her." One holy person in an evil city can actually turn
away God's wrath. One godly individual who cares for
a city (or a family or a school or a neighborhood or a
church) swings open the door for mercy.

If just one soul refuses to give in to the intimidation
of increasing wickedness, if that one refuses to submit to
hopelessness, fear or unbelief, it is enough to exact from
heaven a delay on wrath. *You*, my friend, can be that one
who obtains forgiveness for your city until revival
comes!

Mercy far outweighs wrath. Mercy always triumphs
over judgment. You see, whenever a person operates in
intercessory mercy, the tender passions of Christ are
unveiled in the world. Do you want to truly know who
Jesus is? Consider: He ever lives to make intercession;
He is seated at the right hand of God the Father praying
on our behalf (Heb 7:25; Rom 8:34). He is not eagerly
waiting in heaven desiring an opportunity to destroy the
world. He is praying for mercy. This is His nature.

Christ, the second person of the Trinity, is God in His
mercy form. He is God loving the world, dying for its
sins, paying the price of redemption. Christ is the mercy
of God satisfying the justice of God.

When God declared that man was to be made in the
divine image, it is this image of Christ the Redeemer that

reveals our pattern. We are to follow the mercy path set by Christ. The Bible says to us, "as He is, so also are we in this world" (1 John 4:17).

Thus, the nature of Christ is manifest in our world every time redemptive intercession is offered to God on behalf of sinners. Jesus came to earth to fulfill the mercy of God. His title is Redeemer. His role is Savior. He is the Good Shepherd who lays down His life for His sheep. God calls us to be like Jesus, who says to us, "as the Father has sent Me, I also send you" (John 20:21). We are sent by Jesus with the purpose of redemption.

The manifestation on earth of one Christlike intercessor perfectly restrains God's need for judgment on a society. Let me say it again: "Mercy triumphs over judgment" (James 2:13). Mercy plays exactly into God's heart. And one man or woman who reveals Christ's heart on earth will defer God's judgment from heaven.

Lord Jesus, forgive me for devaluing the power of prayer. Forgive me for underestimating how passionately You desire to reveal Your mercy. Lord, give me grace to be one who never ceases to cry out to You for mercy. Lord, let me not base my obedience on what my eyes see or my ears hear but, upon the revelation of Your mercy, let me build my life on Thee. AMEN!

CHAPTER FIVE

PRAYER
CHANGES
THE MIND OF GOD

LIFE OF THE INTERCESSOR

I n the last chapter we gazed at the effect of mercy on the heart of God: the Lord would spare Sodom for the sake of ten righteous souls. We also discovered that God's mercy would have gone ever further. Even as the Lord's wrath was about to fall on Jerusalem, the Lord said if there had been just one man of integrity in the city, the man's presence could have gained pardon for the entire city (Jer 5:1).

Yet, the Lord's willingness to extend mercy has not always been welcomed by the church. We must rediscover true, basic Christianity. We have been content to possess a religion about what Jesus did without actually manifesting the reality of who Jesus is. Truly, our destiny does not find sure footing until the life of Christ emerges through us.

This Christlike transformation of the church was of the utmost concern for Paul. "My children," he wrote, "with whom I am again in labor until Christ is formed in you" (Gal 4:19). Christianity is nothing less than Christ Himself entering our lives and taking our form.

Again, Paul wrote, this time to the Corinthians:

For we who live are constantly being delivered over to death for Jesus' sake, that the life of Jesus also may be manifested in our mortal flesh.
—2 Cor 4:11

Do we see this? This is basic Christianity: the "life of Jesus . . . manifested in our mortal flesh." Anything less than Jesus' very life revealed through us will never satisfy our thirst to know the substance of God.

When we accepted Christ into our lives, it meant not only that we would gain passage to heaven, but that He could again find passage to earth. Our salvation gives Jesus flesh and blood access for bringing mercy toward the specific needs of our world.

Paul said he was in spiritual travail, "labor," to see the life of Christ formed in the church. What is the life of Christ? To the church in Philippi he explained it this way:

Have this attitude in yourselves which was also in Christ Jesus, who, although He existed in the form of God, did not regard equality with God a thing to be grasped, but emptied Himself, taking the form of a bond-servant, and being made in the likeness of men. And being found in appearance as a man, He humbled Himself by becoming obedient to the point of death, even death on a cross.   —Phil 2:5–8

Christ is the Redeemer of the world; its Savior. Such characteristics are unfamiliar to us. However, it means we seek for mercy to triumph, for redemption to succeed, and God to be glorified in all things. To attain Christ's mind, God calls us to a realignment of our thoughts, attitudes and motives until we think and act in perfect synchrony with Christ's nature.

We will not arrive at this overnight; it is a lifetime pursuit. Yet it means we set our goal not to be judgmental but redemptive in our motives. We shun personal ambition and self-righteousness, replacing them with humility and love-motivated courage.

Think of it: We have been granted access to, or possession of, the very mind of Christ! This is not a *doctrinally* based mind, but a *mercy*-based view of life. An entirely new paradigm born of Christ's redemptive motive is destined to arise in those who seek Christlikeness.

Consider: From His vantage point of "equality with God" in eternity, Christ saw the world in all its sinfulness. He beheld the very worst of man's blood lust and immorality. The Lord beheld the long Dark Ages that blanketed Christianity. He contemplated the carnage of hundreds of wars throughout time, and specifically the two great wars that stormed through our world this past century. He knew there would be abortions, ethnic cleansing, witchcraft and human sacrifices. He was conscious of the fact that the entertainment industry would exploit man's fallen nature and that there would be those who would dedicate themselves to promoting sexual lust and violence throughout the world.

Having seen the sin that the world would commit, amazingly He did not condemn the world. Instead, He died for it. It is in this regard that Paul urges us, "Have this mind in you which was also in Christ Jesus" (Phil 2:5 KJV). This is the new paradigm: Our perception of the world must conform to what perfect love would do in all things.

How do we know if we have possessed the mind of Christ? Any time mercy-based, intercessory prayer manifests through us, the "mind . . . which was also in Christ Jesus" is functioning through us. Indeed, whenever Christ has a human counterpart praying on earth, Christ's prayer *through His intercessor* becomes the prevailing influence in the Godhead.

INTERCESSION: THE ESSENCE OF CHRIST

Throughout the ages Christ has revealed Himself through the intercession of the saints; the mercy prayer triumphed, whether our examples lived in Old or New Testament times. Was judgment for sin imminent? When Christ was revealed through redemptive intercession, divine wrath was restrained, delayed or even averted. Had Israel become wanton? When mercy pleads for time, though iniquity still abounds, grace abounds even more.

Since the advent of the New Testament, Christ has purposed to raise up an army of Spirit-filled individuals whose prayers and actions multiplied mercy opportunities for the Father. Yet there have *always* been intercessors and visionaries whose prayers turned the heart of God from judgment to mercy. One such individual was Moses.

Moses exemplifies a man growing through the stages of intercession. Although he was born an Israelite, as an infant he was taken by Pharaoh's daughter and raised as an Egyptian.

During his first forty years, Moses was "educated in all the learning of the Egyptians" and became a man "of power in words and deeds" (Acts 7:22).

As he matured, however, a time came when he could no longer remain detached from the sufferings of his Israelite brethren; he began to identify with the people of God. Here is how the book of Hebrews renders this transition in Moses' life:

> By faith Moses, when he had grown up, refused to be called the son of Pharaoh's daughter; choosing rather to endure ill-treatment with the people of God, than to enjoy the passing pleasures of sin.   —Heb 11:24–25

The Scriptures explain that when we number ourselves with others in need we are actually, in some fashion, revealing the nature of Christ (see Isa 53). Hebrews 11:26 confirms this, saying that when Moses chose to endure ill-treatment with the people of God, he was, in fact, bearing "the reproach of Christ."

Christ is God; He is the fullness of the Godhead in bodily form and thus, beyond reproach. However, the reproach Christ bears comes from His identification with sinners. The Pharisees reproached Christ because He accepted the ungodly into His company. Moses united himself with the humiliation and dehumanization of his brethren, who were slaves in Egypt. Yet, in so doing, he discovered that the reproach of Christ was "greater riches than the treasures of Egypt" (Heb 11:26).

The quickening in Moses was actually a Christ awakening. However, though Moses was awakened spiritually, he had not yet been trained. He was still immature and unfamiliar with the ways of God. His heart was open to Christ, but his mind was still in control of his decisions; in presumption he murdered an Egyptian. The Lord will not reject us for our fleshly beginnings, but neither will He endorse them. They invariably fail to bring deliverance.

Moses fled and spent forty years in the wilderness. There, alone with God, his pride and self-will were broken. Indeed, without brokenness no man can serve the Lord. Brokenness is openness to God. When the Lord finally sent Moses back, he went with true power as the leader of Israel and its intercessor.

What is a spiritual leader? He is one who is given the task of bringing God's promise to an imperfect people, and then he remains committed in prayer for that people until God's promise comes to pass. This is the nature of true intercession. Though we may indeed hate the sin that holds people in bondage, we cannot despise people for their rebellion and unbelief; this is the very reason they need our prayer!

Throughout Israel's long wilderness journey, Moses positions himself between the imminent judgment of God and God's mercy. Over and over again, he secures forgiveness from the Almighty which allows the people of Israel, even in their imperfections, to move forward. Throughout the entire journey Moses stays before God, never abandoning his role as intercessor; never doubting God's willingness to forgive the people. Remember, his task is to bring an imperfect people from "promise to fulfillment."

Moses himself was not perfect or immune to his own fleshly reactions. Frequently, he had to deal with Israel's criticism of himself and Aaron. Often, the Israelites fell into unbelief, murmuring and complaining against him, and he grew angry. Yet, he never failed to deal with his attitude and return to prayer for Israel.

At the same time, Moses himself was learning God's ways. An important lesson came when Amalek rose up to war against Israel. Moses said to Joshua,

"Choose men for us, and go out, fight against Amalek. Tomorrow I will station myself on the top of the hill with the staff of God in my hand." And Joshua did as Moses told him, and fought against Amalek; and Moses, Aaron, and Hur went up to the top of hill.

So it came about when Moses held his hand up, that Israel prevailed, and when he let his hand down, Amalek prevailed. But Moses' hands were heavy. Then they took a stone and put it under him, and he sat on it; and Aaron and Hur supported his hands, one on one side and one on the other. Thus his hands were steady until the sun set. So Joshua overwhelmed Amalek and his people with the edge of the sword.

—Ex 17:9–13

Moses realized that Israel's victory was attached to his posture before God. As leaders and intercessors, the victory that God's people are reaching for is often, in some measure, attached to our stand before God. The position of leaders in the "prayer posture" will add power and victory to the people in the "fight posture."

There are marriages in your neighborhood that are going to have a breakthrough because you stand before God with your hands lifted in prayer. There are breakthroughs in schools that will come, not because anyone is doing anything differently, but because you have placed yourself before God and are in prayer. Police will arrest criminals quicker because the church lifts its hands in prayer. The person who stands before God and prays is valuable to God and instrumental in gaining the victory.

Years ago I pastored a small church. Almost without fail, each night I would pray for the congregation before I went to sleep. One night, however, I forgot to pray. Seven-thirty the next morning I received a call: One of the men in the church had been in a serious accident. Immediately I thought, "I did not pray last night," but then I dismissed it. I did not want to accept that my lack of prayer could have in any way contributed to what happened.

About six months later, again I went to sleep without praying for the church. And again, the next morning I woke to a distressing phone call. One of the farmers in the church had been harvesting when both his feet were caught and mangled in a jammed auger. Again, I thought, "I didn't pray last night," but once more I did not want to accept that people's lives could be left vulnerable by my lack of prayer. Still, the fear of God was on me because of these two accidents, so I made a more committed effort to intercede for my congregation nightly.

The following summer I spoke at a Christian camp and brought my family with me. My youngest son asked me to lie down with him that night. Exhausted, I laid down next to him and instantly we both fell asleep. When I came home from the camp I had another phone call waiting: A young woman in the church had rolled her car and crashed into a ditch. I knew the Lord was revealing to me something that I could no longer resist accepting: *my lack of prayer left people vulnerable to the enemy.*

Although all three of these people recovered from their injuries, I have never recovered from not praying at night. I often find myself waking in the middle of the night, interceding for various individuals or situations. As a leader or intercessor, God gives us spiritual authority to protect those whom we love. As wide as our range of love, to that degree we have authority in prayer. Such is the unique place we have, whether we are praying for our family, our church, city or nation, people will receive certain victories and protection that they otherwise would not have.

Let me share another example about the power of intercession to protect people. Several years ago, for a period of two weeks, pastors gathered each weekday at noon for prayer; we were specifically praying for our city and our local mayor. During this time our mayor and his wife came to Christ and each made a radical commitment to serve Him. However, within the next four months the enemy challenged the direction God was taking the city, and our community experienced three murders. The mayor and a couple of pastors consulted together and it was decided to meet in his office for prayer every Wednesday morning at six a.m. This prayer continued until his term was up (he chose to not run again). But throughout that time and for a year and a half afterwards, there was not another murder in the city—a total of more than thirty months!

When leaders and intercessors pray, God protects.

DON'T LEAVE GOD ALONE!

As we return to our study of Moses, again we see that Israel has sinned, this time constructing a golden calf, an idol, made from their melted jewelry. The Lord spoke to Moses, "Go down at once, for your people, whom you brought up from the land of Egypt, have corrupted themselves" (Ex 32:7). Remember, the glory of God has descended over the whole of Mount Sinai, three million Israelites are encamped at the foot of this mountain and a pillar of fire has settled in blazing glory on the mountain peak. Into this glory, Moses climbed and remained for forty days (Ex 24:18). At first Israel was terrified. Then, when Moses delayed his return, the people made a golden calf to worship as an idol. They lived in full view of the glory of God and then defied God's glory with their idolatry.

The Lord said to Moses,

> "I have seen this people, and behold, they are an obstinate people. Now then let Me alone, that My anger may burn against them, and that I may destroy them; and I will make of you a great nation." —Ex 32:9–10

This is an amazing verse. The Lord says, "Let Me alone." As long as Moses *does not* let God alone, the Lord will not destroy Israel. *This is the only time our direct disobedience brings pleasure to the Lord.* Moses refuses to leave the ear and heart of God. Why? Because if there is one man standing in the gap, God's mercy stays kindled.

The goal of an intercessor is to not let God alone. The goal of the devil is to separate you from standing before God for your family, your city, your church, or your school. If the Lord has no intercessor, potentially His wrath may be kindled. "Let Me alone," the Lord says, yet Moses refuses. He is compelled by God's very mercy to disobey.

Moses has become a mature intercessor: He stays close to God, prevailing in prayer. Even though the Lord says He will make of Moses a great nation, Moses ignores the prospect. He knows that no matter what people he must lead, there will be problems, sin and failure. No, Moses has come too far to start over. And then he reminds the Lord of the promise He made to

Abraham, Isaac and Jacob. This journey is about a covenant that was made with Israel's forefathers.

Remember, the assignment is to bring an imperfect people with a promise from God into fulfillment. The intercessor's role is to pray from the beginning of that journey, through the valleys of sin and setbacks, and continue praying until the promise from God is obtained.

You may be a pastor of a church or an intercessor or a parent. However, whatever you are praying for, you must have the attitude: *Lord, I am not letting You alone concerning this people.* Never pray for judgment or wrath; always pray for mercy. Such is the heart that brings heaven to earth and fulfillment to promises.

> So the Lord changed His mind about the harm which He said He would do to His people.
> —Ex 32:14

May this be a revelation to us all! *Moses' prayer changed God's mind!*

You may have a rebellious child or a mean-spirited boss or someone in your neighborhood who is pushing everyone to the limit. Instinctively, we desire that God would punish the individual who has wronged us. It is here that we must refuse to take our battles personally. Publicly, Moses was very upset with Israel; privately he pleaded with God for mercy, and he changed God's mind.

This is another reason why Jesus said we will not know the day or the hour when the time of great judgment would begin, because prayer can change the mind of God. In fact, Jesus tells us to "pray that your flight may not be in the winter" (Matt 24:20). We minimize it, but prayer actually can influence the season when the Great Tribulation begins.

Much of how God relates to a nation, city, church, or group is based upon how the people in that society pray. Prayer or lack of prayer sits at the table in the counsel of God's will. For Moses and the Israelites the outcome was profound: "So the Lord changed His mind about the harm which He said He would do to His people." Think of it: prayer changed God's mind.

Lord, thank You for always remaining entreatable to our cry. Help me to persevere, to give You no rest, until You fulfill Your highest purposes with my nation. Thank You that one voice is not too feeble that You cannot hear it, but that You will respond even to one intercessor who stands with You for the cause of mercy.

CHAPTER SIX

PARDON FOR AN UNREPENTANT PEOPLE

"ACCORDING TO YOUR WORD"

M oses sent twelve spies to Canaan to bring back a report of the land. When they returned, ten said that, though the land was good, Israel would surely be defeated by the inhabitants. Although Joshua and Caleb argued that Israel certainly could drive out their enemies, the people moaned, complained, and rebelled, even seeking to stone Joshua and Caleb and return with new leaders to Egypt. And again, the anger of the Lord was kindled against them and threatened to bring judgment (see Num 12–14).

Faithfully, once more Moses intercedes.

"I pray, let the power of the Lord be great, just as Thou hast declared. The Lord is slow to anger and abundant in lovingkindness, forgiving iniquity and transgression; but He will by no means clear the guilty, visiting the iniquity of the fathers

on the children to the third and the fourth genera-
tions."   —Num 14:17–18

Just as Abraham had prayed centuries before, Moses
focuses upon two things: the integrity of the Lord and
His great mercy. When the Scripture says He will "by no
means clear the guilty," it speaks of those who sin yet do
not repent. Yet, even here the Lord is able to be en-
treated.

Remember, the Israelites have rebelled; they are not
even aware that their sin has them at the threshold of
God's wrath. The Lord looks at a nation of unrepentant,
sinful people on one side and one man, Moses, praying
on the other. Even though Moses acknowledges that the
Lord will not "clear the guilty," Moses still prays that
God would forgive Israel,

> "Pardon, I pray, the iniquity of this people ac-
> cording to the greatness of Thy lovingkindness,
> just as Thou also hast forgiven this people, from
> Egypt even until now."   —Num 14:19

Listen in awe at the Lord's response to Moses' mercy
prayer. He says, "I have pardoned them according to your
word" (Num 14:20).

Incredible!

Three million Israelites had not repented, nor rent
their hearts, nor confessed their sins to God and one
another. Not one of them who sinned possessed a broken,
contrite spirit. Yet, the Lord says, "I have pardoned
them." This is utterly amazing to me. The Lord granted
Israel forgiveness "according to [Moses'] word."

Staggering!

One man with favor from God brought mercy upon three million people who had not repented.

Then, in case we think this is some kind of easy grace, the Lord reaffirms His purpose with all nations, beginning with Israel. He says, "But indeed, as I live, all the earth will be filled with the glory of the Lord" (Num 14:21).

The integrity of the Lord is non-negotiable. He says, in effect, *though I forgive, I am not going to change My plans. All the earth will be filled with My glory.*

When we ask God for mercy, we are not asking Him to compromise His intentions. We are only asking that He forgive the sins of people until He can fulfill His purpose. In truth, we are in complete agreement with His desire. We earnestly want His glory to overshadow America, to fall upon Canada, to roll through Europe and Asia, Israel and the Middle East—all over the world, in fact. We shout a resounding "Yes!" to the purpose of God. Fill our land with Your glory, Lord. Fill Canada. Flood South and Central America. Drench Europe, Israel and Africa, Asia and Australia with Your majestic glory. But we also pray: Until Your purposes are perfected, reveal Your mercy and forgive the sins of Your people.

Do you need a vision of God's ultimate destiny for your nation? The Lord swore, "as I live, all the earth will be filled with . . ." Your nation is included in God's heart. He will hear our prayer for mercy as we reach, with Him, toward His ultimate goal.

Do you doubt this? *The mercy prayer worked for Moses.* God brought the first of His nations, Israel, from

Egypt to Canaan, and He did so through the prayer and leadership of one man.

You say, "But that was Moses. I am a nobody." Jesus said, "He who is least in the kingdom of heaven is greater" than the greatest prophets in the Old Testament (see Matt 11:11). How can that be? We have the power of Christ's blood covenant to aid our quest for mercy!

Yes, God indeed used Moses to bring an imperfect people from promise to fulfillment. Whether we are praying for our nation, our cities, our churches, or our family, the Lord will "pardon them according to your word."

An Intercessor is Committed

Then Moses returned to the Lord, and said, "Alas, this people has committed a great sin, and they have made a god of gold for themselves. But now, if Thou wilt, forgive their sin—and if not, please blot me out from Thy book which Thou hast written!" —Ex 32:31–32

An intercessor gives up all personal advantage for the sake of those he prays for. Moses knows he has favor with God. Yet, he presents himself as a remarkable portrait of one irreversibly committed to Israel's transformation. He says, "If thou wilt, forgive their sin—and if not, please blot me out from Thy book."

Moses is saying, in effect, that he is not serving for individual gain or glory. This servant of the Lord cannot be separated, blessed, honored, or pleased apart from the fulfillment of God's promise to Israel. If God will not forgive them, He cannot have Moses either. Israel and Moses have become a package deal.

Some have struggled with situations in their personal lives where they cannot seem to break through. Perhaps you are spending too much time on *your* needs and not enough time praying for others. Make a prayer list of people with desperate needs, and as you intercede for them, see if the Holy Spirit doesn't break through for you, too. Remember the story of Job. When he prayed for his friends, God healed him. *Intercession not only transforms the world, it transforms us.*

ONE MORE THOUGHT

Moses accomplished what the Lord gave him to do: Through him, God brought the Israelites from Egypt to the Promised Land.

The book of Psalms records the tremendous role Moses played in bringing Israel from Egypt to the Promised Land:

> They made a calf in Horeb, and worshiped a molten image. Thus they exchanged their glory for the image of an ox that eats grass. They forgot God their Savior, who had done great things in Egypt, wonders in the land of Ham, and awesome things by the Red Sea. Therefore He said that He would destroy them, had not Moses His chosen one stood in the breach before Him, to turn away His wrath from destroying them.
>
> —Ps 106:19–23

One man changed the mind of God.

But something happened on that journey that was not good for Moses. Israel was thirsty. This time, instead of striking the rock to bring water, the Lord told Moses to speak to it. Angered at the people for their sin, Moses struck the rock instead. This action disqualified Moses from entering the Promised Land (see Num 20:8–13).

I have often pondered this situation. Moses went so far, yet could not go with Israel into Canaan. Then it occurred to me, *it is possible Moses couldn't enter the promises because there was no one praying for him in the hour of his sin.*

Everyone needs someone who will pray for them. You need to pray for your pastor, and pray for those who intercede for others. Everyone has at least one place in their heart that is not yet transformed, an area that needs the intercession of Christ to emerge through a friend on their behalf. Even Moses, intercessor for millions, needed someone to pray and stand in the breach of obedience in his own life.

Lord Jesus, I am awed at Your willingness to show mercy. You actually changed Your mind about judgment on sinners because of one man, Moses. Lord, in my world and times, let me be that one who so delights You, who is so intimate with You, that my prayer for mercy outweighs Your need to destroy the unsaved. May the favor You have given to me be multiplied to those who yet do not know You, and may it spread until all the earth is filled with Your glory!

CHAPTER SEVEN

GOD
TALKING TO GOD

W e have been studying the influence that one mercy-motivated intercessor can have upon the heart of God. In this, we looked at Abraham and then expanded our study to Moses. We saw, with amazement, how the Lord heard and responded with mercy to the prayer for mercy. One person, Moses, stood between divine judgment and Israel's sin; and one person's intercession was enough to bring Israel from its confusion as a nation of oppressed, rebellious slaves to becoming the standard of spiritual attainment portrayed in the Old Testament. Let us revel in the power of prayer and the entreatable heart of God.

Yet, even as we are awed by the power and mercy released through prayer, in the subconscious realms of our souls, for some, another thought forms. At first, it appears as a question. However, because it is left unattended, it often mutates into a doubt. Our problem is this: As we watch the cycle repeat itself again and again—of

Israel's sin, of God's threatened wrath and of Moses' plea for mercy—we are troubled: *Is Moses, a mere man, more merciful than God?*

The very idea seems blasphemous; we are instantly ashamed we thought it. So we bury it. Yet, the fact is, for many, the doubt remains alive. For it is true: had not Moses interceded, the Lord would have destroyed men, women and children for one short period of sin. Moses does seem to be more merciful than God.

Of course, as good Christians, we dare not voice this doubt; we do not even whisper it to our most trusted friends. As a result, what ought to be a pure and wonderful example of the value and power of prayer, instead, on a more subconscious level, tempts us to mistrust God's goodness whenever our goodness fails.

Even if you are not personally struggling with this battle, someone you love probably is or will be. When people fall away from God, often it is because they have sinned and now doubt the Lord's goodness to forgive them.

Thus, we need to clear up this mystery concerning God's wrath. Why isn't God *automatically* merciful? Why does He warn of judgment, yet show Himself willing to show mercy and restraint when even one intercessor pleads with Him on behalf of others?

THE PURPOSE OF GOD

To answer these questions we must return to the first statements the Almighty made in Genesis concerning mankind; we must understand the reason for our existence. Let's read as God Himself declared His purpose in the sacred Scriptures. The Lord said,

> "Let Us make man in Our image, according to Our likeness . . . And God created man in His own image, in the image of God He created him; male and female He created them."
>
> —Gen 1:26–27

The Living God has encoded into humanity a grand and irreversible purpose: *Man has been created to reveal the nature of God.* This has been the Lord's purpose from the beginning and, though the world has continually changed, the Almighty has never deviated from this plan.

We should not assume that the creation of Adam and Eve, however, completed this purpose. Genesis marks a beginning, not a fulfillment. Although Adam and Eve possessed intelligence and freedom of will above that of the animals, God's plan was only *initiated* in Eden; they were still far from being in the "image and likeness of God." Indeed, shortly after they were created, they fell into sin. If they were *functionally* created in the likeness of God, how is it that they sin? Sin is the one thing God *cannot* do.

Let's think of mankind as a singular person in search of his identity and destiny. For man, Eden is the commencement to a journey that can only end when man attains the image and likeness of God. Man discovers sin, but fulfillment is not there; he receives moral law and tries to obey it, but again, satisfaction eludes him. Having been born in paradise with God, the man carries in his primordial soul the memory of paradise lost.

The introduction of Christ into the consciousness of mankind marks the beginning, in divine earnest, of God acting to accomplish His original purpose with man. Christ provides payment for man's sins, but He also sets the pattern for man's lives. As Christians we heartily agree with the payment of Christ; however, we only remotely accept the pattern He provides. We think the first aspect of our relationship with Christ, our forgiveness, was the goal. It is not. The first purpose is servant to the second. Christ forgives us so He can transform us.

Man transformed into the image of Christ is the pinnacle truth, the supreme revelation, of God's will for humanity. No truth is more poignantly chronicled by Jesus and the New Testament writers. Every instruction of righteousness points us to the standard of Christ; every apostolic teaching prods us to fulfill Genesis 1:26–27 through the manifestation of Christ within us.

Paul tells us in Romans 8:28–30 that Christ is the first-born of many predestined brethren. Galatians 2:20 and 2 Corinthians 13 explain that Christ is living in us now, while 2 Corinthians 3:18 assures us that, from the moment Christ entered our spirits, as we behold Him we each "are being transformed into the same image from glory to glory, just as from the Lord, the Spirit."

We are born again, not just to go to heaven, but to become like Christ. We unite with other Christians, not only for administrative expediency, but because Christ manifests Himself most perfectly through a many membered body. We are part of a second Genesis whose goal remains to fulfill the first Genesis. In scores of Scriptures, some so sublime their truths are yet to be fully apprehended, the Holy Spirit repeatedly proclaims the magnificent purposes of God in man.

Finally, at the sounding of the last trump of this dispensation, our mortality will put on immortality and our corruption will put on incorruption, and we shall be like Him (1 Cor 15:53; 1 John 3:2). At that moment, all heaven will celebrate in awe and praise, for "the mystery of God is finished" (Rev 10:7). Man, in perfect submission to God, shall bear His glory and power.

Adam never was the prototype. From eternity God's purpose was that man would be conformed to Jesus Christ. God chose us in Christ *prior* to Adam's fall. Indeed, He chose us "before the foundation of the world" (Eph 1:4).

So, God's purpose from the beginning was to make man in Christ's image. When we seek to know God's will, let us seek first to satisfy the call to Christlikeness. Yes, more important than whom will we marry, where will we work or what church we should attend, we must seek to attain and reveal the nature of Christ in all things. To be like Jesus is the reason God created man; it is the reason He created *you.*

LET US MAKE MAN

Yet, we haven't fully addressed the mystery of God, man, and the power and purpose of prayer. All we have done is establish that God's purpose in creating man was to reveal through him the glorious nature of Christ. So let's return to Genesis.

When speaking of the Almighty, we are taught, and so believe, that the "the Lord is one!" (Deut 6:4) The Scriptures nearly always refer to God in *singular* terms. We read that God *(singular)* created the physical world. But then, when we study His creation of man, the Almighty speaks of Himself in *plural* terms, saying, "Let *Us* make man . . ."

We define the Lord's ability to remain one in nature yet separate in manifestation as the Trinity. One clear example is seen in the relationship between Jesus and His Father. Each time Christ prayed to the Father, it was, in truth, God on earth talking with God in heaven: God separating from Himself, yet remaining one with Himself.

Though Jesus Christ bears and represents mankind through the human side of His nature, spiritually He is of the same substance as God. Paul tells us that, "although He existed in the form of God, [He] did not regard equality with God a thing to be grasped, but emptied Himself" (Phil 2:6–7). He is "begotten" of the Father as He enters the realm of time, remaining one with God, yet separated organically from the Godhead by human flesh and subjective human experience. As Christians, we accept the mystery of the Trinity even if we cannot fully understand it.

However, this discovery of God's "separated oneness" leads back to our original question concerning God's judgments, Moses, and the reason for intercessory prayer. Indeed, it explains what the Father seeks to accomplish and why it seems that Moses was more merciful than God.

Let's look at what happened to Moses to bring him into his relationship with the Almighty. We can imagine that the highly cultured Egyptians were shocked that Moses, now a mature and popular prince in Egypt, had become increasingly more concerned for the Hebrew slaves. After all, Moses was enjoying the finest conditions that civilization and position in life provided. There was nothing to gain, no personal advantage to be found, by identifying with Egypt's slaves. The Egyptians deemed the Israelites hardly more valuable than cattle. The idea of somehow helping the Hebrews was preposterous. Help them? As a prince in Egypt, Moses *owned* them!

Yet, Moses could not defend himself against the deepening burdens of his own heart. Even against his will, empathy toward the Hebrews was growing within him. From the moment he began to identify with the weaknesses, the injustices and the sufferings of his oppressed brethren, the Spirit of Christ set about to awaken him to his destiny. As we said earlier, this act of compassionate identification with those who are scorned, disgraced or discredited is called the *reproach of Christ,* which Moses considered to be "greater riches than the treasures of Egypt" (Heb 11:26).

This process of training, breaking and reshaping continued in Moses for forty years. Until Christ began His work in him, Moses had been aloof and apathetic toward Israel's need, but with the introduction of Christ into his life, he became God's vehicle to bring mercy, and extend mercy, to Israel.

Whenever we read of intercessory prayer or redemptive action on the part of one for the needs of many, whether New or Old Testament, it is actually Christ manifesting through that individual. Moses bore *Christ's* reproach and was himself the expression of God's mercy toward Israel.

The question of whether Moses is more merciful than God proves to be superfluous, for the spirit of intercession emerging through Moses is not Moses, but Christ praying through him on man's behalf. This is significant: man is the primary means through which God brings forth mercy to other men. What we actually are seeing operating through human instrumentality is God in His mercy interceding before God in His justice. *At the highest level, intercessory prayer is God talking to God through man.*

Remember, we said earlier that God separates Himself from Himself, yet never loses His essential oneness with Himself in the Godhead. When the Lord appears ready to reveal His wrath, He will always, simultaneously, be searching for an individual through whom Christ can emerge in the mercy prayer. God's goal is not to destroy wickedness, but to transform man into the image of Christ. If threatening justifiable wrath awakens even one to manifest the mercy of Christ, that one transformed life is more valuable to the Almighty than His need to destroy wickedness.

Without a doubt, God *must* reveal His righteous judgment concerning sin; otherwise mercy has no meaning or value. In the Godhead, the Father is revealed as God in authority, perfect in holiness and justice; He sets the standard of perfection. Christ is God revealed in redemptive mercy; He satisfies the Father's standard of righteousness with a law of love that is purer than ritual obedience to the Law. The Holy Spirit is God in manifest power, bringing forth in creative or destructive power the expressed will of the Godhead. The ultimate goal of God is to display the divine nature in its highest glory, which is perfect love, and then conform man to that image.

Thus, as Christians, our call is to manifest the voice and mercy of Christ to God. In intercessory prayer and mercy-motivated action, we identify with those exiled from heaven because of sin; we unite with those who feel separated from God because of physical suffering, heartache or persecution. In manifesting the redemptive mercy of God, we embrace the very reason for our existence: to be transformed into Christ's image.

MORE PERFECT THAN PARADISE

God is so committed to man's transformation that He limited much of the administration of mercy to *only* come through human agencies. Yes, He provides the gifts of life and makes His rain to fall on the just and unjust. However, we must feed the hungry and clothe the naked; the oppressed will likely remain so until an anointed man or woman brings deliverance. The suffering in the world around us compels us either toward hardness of heart or compassion. This is the very nature of life itself: God's mercy enters this world through the narrow channel of the human will.

Thus, the Lord tells Moses,

"Behold, the cry of the sons of Israel has come
to Me; furthermore, I have seen the oppression
with which the Egyptians are oppressing them.
Therefore, come now, and I will send you to
Pharaoh."   —Ex 3:9–10

The Lord says, "I have seen the oppression . . . I will
send you." God sees the need, but He reveals His mercy
through His servant. So also with us: God sees the
oppression and hears the cry of people, but His plan of
action is to inspire us to allow Christ to reach through us
to others. Whether we are speaking of Moses' intercession or the temple offerings of the Jewish priests or the
most perfect act of intercession, Christ's incarnation and
death, God's mercy finds its greatest manifestation
through human instrumentality.

When we hear that the Spirit of God is threatening
judgment, the very fact that He warns us gives us the
opportunity, even with fear and trembling, to embrace
the role of Christ-inspired intercession. God actually
desires that we touch His heart with mercy, thus averting
wrath. In truth, the primary reason God warns is not so
we can run and hide, but so we can stand and pray. He
seeks to inspire mercy in His people. Even when the
Almighty shows Himself angered or grieved and poised
for judgment, He tells us that He is still seeking a means
of mercy. He says, "I searched for a man among them
who should . . . stand in the gap before Me for the land,
that I should not destroy it" (Ezek 22:30).

We can expect that the Lord would thrust us into
times of desperation where we would face genuine
calamities or fearful situations. He does this in order that

we truly participate with Him in the redemptive purpose. And it is here, whether our cry is for our children or church, our city or country, that we are compelled toward God for mercy, for it is often in pure desperation that we grasp and attain the nature of Christ.

To turn and actually call or demand divine judgment against people is to position ourselves in an attitude that is exactly *opposite* the heart God desires to reveal in us. Indeed, whenever we judge after the flesh, there is only one thing we can be guaranteed, according to Jesus. He says, "In the way you judge, you will be judged; and by your standard of measure, it will be measured to you" (Matt 7:2). In fact, God will often *stop* dealing with the one we are judging and start dealing with us if our attitude is anything but the redemption of God.

Now, let me state that there will be times when we are called to bring forth God's judgment, but there is a prerequisite. John says,

> And we have come to know and have believed the love which God has for us. God is love, and the one who abides in love abides in God, and God abides in him.
>
> By this, love is perfected with us, that we may have confidence in the day of judgment; because as He is, so also are we in this world.
>
> —1 John 4:16–17

There is a time when God brings forth judgment, not only in the final sense, but in the immediacy of our world. The word *confidence* in this context means "free speech." In other words, not until "love is perfected with us" will we qualify to speak God's wrath. Possessing God's love precedes proclaiming God's judgments.

Adam's sin and subsequent expulsion from Eden seemed the worst of all possible events; yet, to the Almighty, there were lessons man needed to learn about mercy and love that could not be taught in Paradise. Indeed, what looks like an imperfect environment to us is actually the perfect place to create man in the likeness of God. Here, we have a realm suitable for producing tested virtue. In this fallen world, character can be proven genuine and worship made pure and truly precious. Yes, it is here where we truly discover the depths of God's love in sending Christ to die for our sins. And here, in the fire of life-and-death realities, is where we become like Him.

Lord Jesus, Your love, Your sacrifice, is the pattern for my life. How I desire to be like You. I want more than anything to reveal Your mercy, both to the world and also to the Father. I surrender all my other rights and privileges that I may possess this glorious gift of conformity to You. I love You, Lord. Use me, pray through me, love through me until, in all things, I reflect Your image and likeness.

CHAPTER EIGHT

THE BELOVED

W e have been talking about prayer, Christlikeness, and the future of our nations. I would like to continue that focus, but look at the manifestation of Christ on earth as it impacts the Father. There is something utterly pleasing to the Father when Christ is revealed. It actually goes far beyond not destroying the wicked; it touches His heart in the depths of His nature.

Thus, to satisfy God, we must perceive what the Son presents to the Father in terms of their relationship. Let us, therefore, consider first the weightiness of having Jesus Christ as our mediator with God.

Jesus says that the Father has loved Him from "before the foundation of the world" (John 17:24). The love that exists between the Father and the Son transcends the boundaries of time. Before the ages began or the stars were young; before the earth, man or angels were created, the Father and Son have known only love. Their union within the Trinity is so complete that, though they are two distinct personalities, the Scripture can state with perfect fidelity: "The Lord our God is one God."

During His ministry, Jesus spoke frequently of this love between the Father and Himself. He said, "The Father loves the Son, and has given all things into His hand" (John 3:35). Again we read, "For the Father loves the Son, and shows Him all things that He Himself is doing" (John 5:20). And again, "I love the Father, and as the Father gave Me commandment, even so I do" (John 14:31).

In Jesus' first public appearance, this love between Father and Son engulfed the scene at the river Jordan. While Jesus was still in the water:

Heaven was opened, and the Holy Spirit descended upon Him in bodily form like a dove, and a voice came out of heaven, "Thou art My beloved Son, in Thee I am well-pleased."
—Luke 3:21–22

Do not rush past this phrase: "My beloved Son." Jesus is not just "a son," or even "the Son," He is the Father's *"beloved* Son." There is no one like Him. Here, in this incredible, inaugural moment, the Father Himself draws near. Almighty God moves from His throne in the highest heaven until His face is at the edge of our physical world. From eternity the Father speaks to His Son: "In Thee I am well-pleased."

Then, the Almighty turns and repeats the identical thought to John the Baptist, the forerunner of Christ: "This is My beloved Son, in whom I am well-pleased" (Matt 3:17).

Note: in both times that He spoke, the Father could not help but express His love for Jesus. In truth, the Father is consumed with love for His Son.

We do not have a human reference to understand the energy, the passion, and the unrestrained oneness that exists between the Father and the Son. We can only stand and watch in awe, and learn of it. It is the essence of heaven; it is the nectar of eternal life.

"Beloved . . . in Thee I am well-pleased."

The deep, unfathomable perfection of God, the incomprehensible ethos of the divine nature, knows only pleasure in Jesus. The Almighty, who gives to all life, receives life from the Son and is fulfilled to the depth of His being. The Father gazes at His Son and harbors no slight shadow of regret, no lingering wish for someone or something to be done better. We behold God on earth satisfying God in heaven: perfect surrender in the embrace of perfect acceptance.

Their relationship is amazing. Yet, add to it the fact that, prior to this encounter, Jesus had not accomplished any miracles; there were no signs or wonders, no vast multitudes. Outwardly, a carpenter named Jesus came, like everyone else, to be baptized. Until that moment, Jesus' life was unremarkable. He was just another woodworker.

How was it that, even in the common tasks of an ordinary life, Jesus drew the praise of heaven? At the core of His being, He only did those things which pleased the Father. In everything, He stayed true, heartbeat to heartbeat, with the Father's desires. Jesus lived for God alone; God was enough for Him. Thus, even in its simplicity and moment-to-moment faithfulness, Christ's life was an unending fragrance, a perfect offering of incomparable love to God.

Privately, the unfolding stream of divine passion from the Father for Jesus never abated; the Jordan was but the first public exchange. We see other references as we proceed through the Scriptures. Look at Matthew's account, chapter 12. Christ's public ministry has begun. Listen to how that which was written from eternity past again describes their holy relationship. Many are following and He is healing them all, yet He bids the multitudes to not make Him known.

> In order that what was spoken through Isaiah the prophet, might be fulfilled, saying, "Behold, My Servant whom I have chosen; My beloved in whom My soul is well-pleased; I will put My Spirit upon Him, and He shall proclaim justice to the Gentiles."   —Matt 12:17–18

Listen to the sacred text, the prophetic word chosen to describe the Father and His beloved. God cannot speak of Christ, or even make reference to Him, without calling Him "My beloved in whom My soul is well-pleased."

One day, indeed, we will gaze upon the face of God's beloved and we will know that to see His face is the highest blessedness of heaven.

Again, look in Matthew 17. On the holy mountain Jesus was magnificently transfigured before three of His disciples. His face shone like the sun. His garments became white as light, flashing like lightning. Moses and Elijah appeared, talking with Christ. Into this splendor, Peter nervously presented an idea. While he was still speaking, a radiant cloud formed and then overshadowed the disciples. Out from this living splendor, again, the voice of God was heard:

"This is My beloved Son, with whom I am well-pleased; listen to Him!"   —Matt 17:5

The all-knowing, all-wise God, the Creator of heaven and earth, in the only times He has ever spoken audibly to mankind, has said the same thing three times: "This is My beloved Son." In all the unlimited creativity of the mind of God, there is nothing more profound, no greater revelation than to say, "Listen to Him!"

In each occasion that He speaks, the Father returns to glorifying His beloved. We hear this information, we write it down, we think we grasp God's truth; but we do not. We underline but do not understand. Too quickly we seek to move to another insight, but the voice of God brings us back. In the Father's eyes, there is no other truth. We have not genuinely understood who Jesus is, otherwise we would feel as the Father does.

This love within the Godhead is the symphony of the universe. It is what makes heaven heavenly. Even as we are awed by such all-consuming oneness, Jesus asks that each of us, as His disciples, would be included in this holy hymn of heaven. He prays,

"O righteous Father . . . I have made Thy name known to them, and will make it known; that the love wherewith Thou didst love Me may be in them, and I in them."   —John 17:25–26

Jesus prays that the same love, the same overwhelming fulfillment that the Father has in His Son, may also be manifested in us. In other words, God desires that *we* become as totally consumed with Jesus as is the Father!

WHAT CHRIST PROVIDES

But this is a book about intercession for our nations. How, then, does the love between the Father and the Son connect us to our homeland and praying for its need?

To answer that, let me pose this question: What is it, uniquely, that the Father has found in the Son that so fulfills Him? I believe the Son's gift is this: Jesus presents to the Father the opportunity to satisfy His deepest passions and to reveal His highest glory, the nature of which is love.

We see this in Jesus' statement, "For this reason the Father loves Me, because I lay down My life" (John 10:17). The Son presents to the Father reconciliation between heaven and earth. He allows God to be revealed as He truly is: not a harsh judge but a loving Father.

Perhaps it is incomprehensible to us that God could suffer or feel pain, yet Scriptures reveal that the Spirit of God relates in interactive union with this world. In His eternal nature, the Father sees man's end from the beginning. However, in His relationship with mankind's journey through time, the Scriptures are plain, the heart of God is vulnerable to humanity.

In Noah's day, we read that the Lord was "grieved in His heart" (see Gen 6:3–6). The Psalms revealed that Israel "grieved Him in the desert" (Ps 78:40). The word *grieved* means to "worry, pain or anger." We know that, when a sinner repents, there is increased joy among angels (Luke 15:7), but what happens in heaven when God is grieved?

You see, the Lord participated vicariously in the suffering of His people. Indeed, in Judges we are told of a time when "He could bear the misery of Israel no longer" (Judges 10:16).

Consider: the Spirit of God was not aloof, separated from Israel's condition. Just as the Spirit hovered over the pre-creation world, so He brooded over Israel, being deeply involved, moved to the point of being unable to "bear the misery of Israel" any longer.

Since mankind's fall, there has been a restless longing in the heart of God toward man. Indeed, if we are unreconciled with someone whom we love, do we not also carry heartache until we are restored? By providing atonement for man's sins, Jesus heals the estrangement, the wound, in the Father's heart, and then He extends that healing to man.

Paul explains what Christ has done in his letter to the Colossians. He writes:

> And when you were dead in your transgressions and the uncircumcision of your flesh, He made you alive together with Him, having forgiven us all our transgressions, having canceled out the certificate of debt consisting of decrees against us and which was hostile to us; and He has taken it out of the way, having nailed it to the cross.
> —Col 2:13–14

Mankind's unpayable debt is paid; God's incurable wound, healed. Not only do we have peace with God through the sacrifice of Christ, God has peace with us. He is freed from the limitations of justice; now He can remove the penalty of sin through love.

Let us celebrate what Christ has done: The demands of divine wrath, which could not be settled by man, are fully settled by God Himself through Christ. God is longing for reconciliation and healing with humanity. Indeed, Jesus said, "The kingdom of heaven may be compared to a certain king who wished to settle accounts" (Matt 18:23). This is God's heart, through Christ: He desires to *settle accounts with mankind!*

As long as we ourselves abide in mercy, the full panorama of divine mercy will remain open and fully active toward mankind's need. When we pray, "in Jesus' name," we are coming to the Father with the goal of mercy in mind. The announcement that we have come "in Jesus' name" signifies we are representatives of Jesus' purpose, which is mercy and not judgment.

COME BOLDLY FOR MERCY!

The Father has never taken pleasure in the death of the wicked. The idea that He has enjoyed destroying sinners is a satanic slander which Christ came to dispel. His attitude toward mankind is exactly the opposite: His joy increases when sinners repent. Because Christ's sacrifice for sin has led millions to repentance, Jesus has increased inestimably the Father's joy.

Because judgment is now atoned for in Christ, the Father has full freedom to consider every prayer for mercy. He no longer is constrained to decide between judgment and mercy: mercy triumphs over judgment!

The church can come boldly into the throne of God's grace and stand before the mercy seat in prayer for the world around us. This is what Jesus gives to the Father: perfect fulfillment of God's love, perfect fulfillment of His compassion, perfect unveiling of the highest glory of God.

In fact, the very inspiration to intercede is the result of Christ working within us. Every time Christ is revealed through our intercession, wrath is delayed and divine mercy begins searching for the opportunity to triumph. When we pray, "God be merciful," we are not merely delaying His wrath; in truth, we are delighting and fulfilling His heart for mercy!

Do you not also feel, increasing in you, the Father's love for Jesus? He brings heaven to earth and bids us to join Him in the redemptive purpose. To cover sin, to not condemn but rather to intercede, is to reveal the nature of Christ. Whenever Christ is revealed, mercy triumphs, and the Father is well-pleased.

Lord Jesus, I desire to join You in bringing pleasure to the Father. Forgive me for my shallowness and indifference. Help me to see in You the pattern of love that never ceased to bring pleasure to the Father. You are the fragrance that pleases God. Come forth in Your mercy, even through me, and make me a source of delight unto the Father. Thank You, Lord, for You are my beloved, too, and in You, I find the river of God's pleasure.

CHAPTER NINE

HE WILL
SPRINKLE
MANY NATIONS

THE GIFT OF WOUNDEDNESS

T he world and all it contains was created for one
purpose: to showcase the grandeur of God's Son.
In Jesus, the nature of God is magnificently and perfectly
revealed; He is the expressed image of God. Yet, to gaze
upon Christ is to also see God's pattern for man. As we
seek to be like Him, we discover that our need was
created for His sufficiency. We also see that, once the
redemptive nature of Christ begins to triumph in our
lives, mercy begins to triumph in the world around us.

How will we recognize revival when it comes?
Behold, here is the awakening we seek: men and women,
young and old, all conformed to Jesus. When will revival
begin? It starts the moment we say "yes" to becoming

like Him; it spreads to others as Christ is revealed through us.

Yet, to embrace Christ's attitude toward mercy is only a first step in our spiritual growth. There are other levels of transformation which call us to deeper degrees of surrender. Indeed, just as Jesus learned obedience through the things He suffered, so also must we (Heb 5:8). And it is here, even while we stand in intercession or service to God, that He gives us the *gift* of woundedness.

"Gift?" you ask. Yes, to be wounded in the service of love, and to remain committed to mercy, is to gain access to power in the redemptive purpose. The steadfast prayer of the wounded intercessor has great influence upon the heart of God.

We cannot become Christlike without experiencing woundedness. You see, even after we come to Christ, we carry encoded within us preset limits concerning how far we will go for love, and how much we are willing to suffer for redemption. The wounding exposes those human boundaries and reveals what we lack of His nature.

The path narrows as we seek true transformation. Indeed, many Christians fall short of Christ's stature because they have been offended. They leave churches discouraged, vowing never again to serve or lead or contribute because, when they offered themselves, their gift was marred by unloving people. To be wounded in the administration of mercy can become a great offense to us, especially as we are waiting for, and even expect, a reward for our good efforts.

Yet, wounding is inevitable if we are following Christ. Jesus was both "marred" and "wounded" (Isa 52:14; Zech 13:6), and we will be as well. How else shall love be perfected?

Beware: Life offers few choices in dealing with our wounds. We either become Christlike and forgive, or we enter a spiritual time warp where we abide continually in the memory of our wounding. Like a systemic disease, it destroys every aspect of our reality. In truth, apart from God, the wounding that life inflicts is incurable; God has decreed: only Christ in us can survive.

Intercessors live on the frontier of change. We are positioned to stand between the need of man and the provision of God. Because we are the agents of redemption, Satan will *always* seek means to offend, discourage, silence or otherwise steal the strength of our prayer. The wounding we receive must be interpreted in light of God's promise to reverse the effects of evil and make them work for good. Since spiritual assaults are inevitable, we must discover how God uses our wounds as the means to greater power. This was exactly how Christ brought redemption to the world.

Jesus knew that maintaining love and forgiveness in the midst of suffering was the key that unlocked the power of redemption. Isaiah 53:11 tells us, "By His knowledge the Righteous One, My Servant, will justify the many, as He will bear their iniquities."

Jesus possessed *revelation knowledge* into the mystery of God. He knew that the secret to unleashing world-transforming power was found at the cross. The terrible offense of the cross became the place of redemption for the world. Yet, remember, Jesus calls us to a cross as well. Wounding is simply an altar upon which our sacrifice to God is prepared.

Listen again to Isaiah's prophetic description of Jesus' life. He says something that at first seems startling, but as we read we discover a most profound truth concerning the power of woundedness. He writes:

> But the Lord was pleased to crush Him, putting Him to grief; if He would render himself as a guilt offering, He will see His offspring, He will prolong His days, and the good pleasure of the Lord will prosper in His hand.   —Isa 53:10

How did Jesus obtain the power of God's pleasure and have it prosper in His hands? During His times of crushing, woundedness and devastation, instead of retaliating, He rendered Himself "as a guilt offering."

The crushing is not a disaster; it is an opportunity. Yet, the greater benefit ascends beyond the effect mercy has upon the sinner; it's the effect our mercy has on *God*. We want to be instruments of God's good pleasure; it is redemption, not wrath, which must prosper in our hands.

So, when Christ encounters conflict, even though He is the Lion of Judah, He comes as the Lamb of God. Even when He is outwardly stern, He is always mindful that, encoded into His DNA, He is the guilt offering. Thus, Jesus not only asks the Father to forgive those who have wounded Him, He numbers Himself *with* the transgressors and intercedes *for* them (see Isa 53:12). He does this because the Father takes no pleasure in the death of the wicked, and it is the pleasure of God that Jesus seeks.

Is this not the wonder and mystery, yes, and the power of Christ's cross? In anguish and sorrow, wounded in heart and soul, still He offered Himself for His executioner's sins. Without visible evidence of success, as an apparent failure before man, He courageously held true to mercy. In the depth of terrible crushing, He let love attain its most glorious perfection as He uttered the immortal words: "Father, forgive them; for they do not know what they are doing" (Luke 23:34).

Christ could have escaped. He told Peter as the Romans came to arrest Him, "Do you think that I cannot appeal to My Father, and He will at once put at My disposal more than twelve legions of angels?" (Matt 26:53) In less than a heartbeat the skies would have been flooded with thousands of warring angels. Yes, Jesus could have escaped, but mankind would have perished. Christ chose to go to hell for us rather than return to heaven without us. Instead of condemning mankind, He rendered *Himself* as the guilt offering. He prays the mercy prayer, "Father, forgive them . . ."

Jesus said, "He who believes in Me, the works that I do shall he do also" (John 14:12). We assume He meant that we would work His miracles, but Jesus did not limit His definition of "works" to the miraculous. The works He did—the redemptive life, the mercy cry, the identification with sinners, rendering Himself a guilt offering—*all* the works He did, we shall "do also."

Thus, because He lives within us, we see that Isaiah 53 does not belong exclusively to Jesus; it also becomes the blueprint for Christ in us. Indeed, was this not part of His reward, that He would see His offspring? (Isa 53:10) True Christians are the progeny of Christ.

Listen to Paul's heart,

Now I rejoice in my sufferings for your sake, and in my flesh I do my share on behalf of His body (which is the church) in filling up that which is lacking in Christ's afflictions.   —Col 1:24

What does the apostle mean? Did not Christ fully pay mankind's debts once for all? Is he implying that *we* now take *Jesus'* place? No. We will never take Jesus' place. *It means that Jesus has come to take our place.* The Son of God manifests all the aspects of His redemptive, sacrificial life through us. Indeed, "As He is, so also are we in this world" (1 John 4:17).

Not only does Paul identify with Christ in his personal salvation, he is consumed with Christ's purpose. He wrote,

That I may know Him, and the power of His resurrection and the fellowship of His sufferings, being conformed to His death.   —Phil 3:10

What a wondrous reality: this *fellowship* of His sufferings. Here, in choosing to yoke our existence with Christ's purpose, we find true friendship with Jesus. This is intimacy with Christ. The sufferings of Christ are not the sorrows typically endured by mankind; they are the afflictions of love. They bring us closer to Jesus as, together, we bring pleasure to God.

Listen to one more thought. The power of Christ is enough to cleanse and turn nations to God. Isaiah 53 is preceded by a grand announcement which heralds the effects of Christ's victory. It reads:

Behold, My servant will prosper, He will be high and lifted up, and greatly exalted.

Just as many were astonished at you, My people, so His appearance was marred more than any man, and His form more than the sons of men.

Thus He will sprinkle many nations, kings will shut their mouths on account of Him; for what had not been told them they will see, and what they had not heard they will understand.

—Isa 52:13–15

What does it mean, that He will "sprinkle many nations?" Under the Old Covenant, priests would take the blood of a sacrificed animal and, with it, sprinkle the temple and its furnishings. By so doing they cleansed and made holy that which was otherwise common and unclean. In the New Testament, every believer serves as a priest before the throne of God (Rev 1:6). We come to sprinkle that which is unclean in our world with the blood of Christ. God promises that, as Christ is revealed through us, the sacrifice of God's Lamb will sprinkle many nations; kings will see and understand.

Our call is to follow the Lamb through our personal woundedness into the triumph of love and redemption. In the area of woundedness, we ask not for wrath, but mercy. Whatever the issue—slander, unfaithfulness, desertion, rejection, racism or abuse—we render ourselves to God. The greater the pain in releasing and forgiving the sins against you, the purer your love becomes. Remember, the prayer of the wounded intercessor holds great sway upon God's heart.

What we become in our individual conformity to Christ may be, in its own way, even more important to God than the revival for which we are praying. Listen, my friends: Just as mankind shall look upon Him whom they pierced, and Christ's wounds shall be with Him forever (Zech 12:10), so *our* wounds will be recognized for what they are: entry points through which Christ's "eternal weight of glory" emanate through us (2 Cor 4:17).

In speaking both of the sprinkling of the nations as well as the manifestation of the Redeemer's life, Isaiah presents a question. He asks, "Who has believed our message? And to whom has the arm of the Lord been revealed?" (Isa 53:1) I write as one who has believed the report. The Scriptures tell us that love "bears all things, believes all things, hopes all things, endures all things. Love never fails" (1 Cor 13:7–8). Yes, when Christ is revealed through the church, the power of redemption will prevail for our land, and mercy will certainly triumph over judgment.

Lord Jesus, for You I live; to be like You, may I be willing to die. Let redemption exult through me! Let mercy triumph through me! Do not allow me to withdraw from the fire of conformity to You. Create me in Your holy image, let love prevail through me!

CHAPTER TEN

A WORLD
IN REVIVAL
AND HARVEST

We all know what the world looks like today: immorality is rampant; abortion, legal; violence, a way of life. Many of the nations we are praying for are considered by sociologists to be in a "post-Christian" era. But I'd like to consider them in pre-revival conditions. Picture your nation on fire for God and the impact it will have on civilization.

I do not mean a revival merely of emotional religion, but a deep revival, born of genuine Christlikeness in the church. Picture your country experiencing a Christ awakening, where a priesthood of mature believers join the Lamb before the throne of God's grace; where the Lamb is offered as a sacrifice for sin and many nations, according to Scripture, are sprinkled and cleansed (see Isa 52).

Do not say it cannot happen. Look at Argentina; consider regions of China and Africa. Imagine your country leading many nations in reconciliation and healing, holiness and the fear of the Lord among the people. Think of the multitudes of non-Christian peoples you would reach with the love of Jesus. Envision a hundred thousand praying, loving missionaries, empowered by the Holy Spirit, being sent from your land to heal and encourage nations on every level of society.

We can go the way of the judgmental and critical. We can listen to those without vision who, like Samson, seek to pull your land down upon themselves and their enemies. Or, we can become Christlike and see a worldwide harvest before Jesus comes.

Remember, God is not looking impatiently at His watch, He's listening to His heart. He takes no pleasure in the death of the wicked; He desires for all men to be saved (2 Pet 3:9). He has made provision for all men at the cross (2 Cor 5:21). He inspired revival before. He can do it again.

Do you remember the story of the demonized boy whose father pleaded with Jesus for help? The man approached Christ feeling defeated, almost hopeless, weary with fighting to keep the boy alive after repeated demonic attacks. The man asked Jesus, "If You can do anything, take pity on us and help us" (Mark 9:22).

Our attitude is often like that of this man. Our shoulders are hunched from fasting and we are wearied with the fight. We come to the Lord looking for pity instead of power; we're seeking comfort instead of conviction to take a stand for our land.

To ask for mere pity from a God who has given us "everything pertaining to life and godliness" is an insult (2 Pet 1:3). Jesus retorted, "If You can! All things are possible to him who believes!" (Mark 9:23)

ALL THINGS ARE POSSIBLE!

Let Christ's words become our battle cry. "With God," Jesus said, "all things are possible" (Matt 19:26). Lay aside the weight of unbelief; there is a race to be run and we can win it. Ask God for more love, for love believes all things, hopes all things and endures all things.

We are in the season of the miraculous. Who would have thought beforehand that the USSR would fall and millions would come to Christ in that nation? Who would have predicted that *hundreds of millions* would have come to Christ just in the last ten years?

As I said, I serve the Lord in the United States: Who would have thought after listening to those who said this nation was doomed that we would see such major decreases in crime, divorce, abortion, and teen pregnancy? Today, there is a resurgence of moral values on college campuses around the U.S. Did we expect this good news? Did we anticipate that a deep and wonderful revival would hit the sports world so that *hundreds* of Christian athletes would become role models for our youth or that whole teams would huddle together in public prayer after games?

Who saw ten years ago that the church in America would be uniting in prayer? Or that reconciliation between races and denominations would begin in earnest? Or that nearly a million and a half men would stand in repentance for America at our national capitol? These things are happening in my land, a mere sign of the good things to come. Greater things can happen in your country. It would be just like the Lord to take your nation and pour out His Spirit upon it!

Daniel said, "The people who know their God will display strength and take action" (Dan 11:32). He went on to say, "Those who have insight will shine brightly like the brightness of the expanse of heaven, and those who lead the many to righteousness, like the stars forever and ever" (Dan 12:3). It is not a time for fear, but faith. We do not need to come beggarly to Christ for pity; He is extending to us His power through our prayers, as long as we don't give up.

Have you heard the story of the man who was driving home from work one day and stopped to watch a local Little League baseball game in a park near his home. He sat down behind the bench on the first baseline and asked one of the boys what the score was.

"We're behind fourteen to nothing," the little boy answered with a smile.

"Really," he said. "I have to say you don't look very discouraged."

"Discouraged," the boy asked with a puzzled look on his face, "why should we be discouraged? We haven't been up to bat yet."

It is not time to be discouraged. I believe the devil has run up the score, but really, we haven't been to bat yet. For much of the past thirty years, we have been playing a poor defense to the devil's initiatives (some of us weren't even playing, but sitting quietly on the bench!). But, my friends, the devil's turn is nearly over, the church is getting ready to step up to the batter's box.

I make no apologies for believing as I do. Even if your country briefly turns darker spiritually, I am fully convinced that, if the church will reveal the nature of Christ, "nations will come to your light, and kings to the brightness of your rising" (Isa 60:3). Yes, the church in the image of Christ can delay God's wrath and release revival in your land.

Other books by Francis Frangipane distributed by New Wine Ministries

The Three Battlegrounds
New Wine Press
An in-depth view of the three areas of spiritual warfare: the mind, the Church and the heavenly places

In the Presence of God
(Holiness, Truth and the Presence of God)
New Wine Press
A penetrating study of the human heart and how God prepares it for His glory.

The Days of His Presence
New Wine Press
As the day of the Lord draws near, the out-raying of Christ's Presence shall arise and appear upon His people!

The House of the Lord
New Wine Press
Pleads God's case for a Christlike Church as the only hope for our cities. It takes a citywide church to win the citywide war.

The Stronghold of God
Creation House
A road map into the shelter of the Most High. The atmosphere of thanksgiving, praise, faith and love are places of immunity for God's servant.

The Power of Covenant Prayer
Creation House
Takes the reader to a position of victory over witchcraft and curses. A must for those serious about attaining Christlikeness.

Discipleship Training Booklets
Arrow Publications

> *A Time to Seek God*
> *Prevailing Prayer Repairers of the Breach*
> *By Wisdom the House Is Built*
> *The Arm of Love*
> *The Baptism of Love*
> *Exposing the Accuser of the Brethren*
> *Discerning of Spirits*
> *The Jezebel Spirit*

By Denise Frangipane

> *Deliverance From PMS*
> *Overcoming Fear!*